GRENADE IN MOUTH

Some Poems of Miyó Vestrini

Chicago: Kenning Editions

GRENADE IN MOUTH

Translation by Anne Boyer & Cassandra Gillig
Research and translation assistance by Faride Mereb
Edited by Faride Mereb and Elisa Maggi
Copyediting by Valentina Mendoza

Cover design and lettering by Faride Mereb
Typography: Trade Gothic, Avenir & Optima Nova

Interior composition by Patrick Durgin
Typography: Avenir Next & Caslon

ISBN: 978-0-9997198-3-1
Library of Congress Control Number: 2018955416

First edition of *Es una buena máquina* © 2014 by Letra Muerta

GRENADE IN MOUTH

LA CIVILIZACION DESCANSA SOBRE LA TRADUCCION

¿Quién traduce? ¿Por qué? ¿Cómo lo hace? Al abrir este dossier sobre la traducción, surgen discusiones que van mucho más allá de la simple equivalencia verbal de un idioma a otro. Primero fue la traducción, después el original, es una de las conclusiones sorprendentes, desconcertantes. Julieta Sucre y Juan Luis Delmont-Mauri, inmersos en el laberinto de Lacan y traductores empedernidos, dialogan apasionadamente sobre el tema. Francisco Rivera, autor de la magistral traducción de cien poemas de Cavafy, expone su propia relación con otras lenguas, en términos de un amor absoluto. Alfredo Silva Estrada explica cómo desde hace años, descifra la gran poesía y la trae al español. Antonio López Ortega establece fronteras propias entre la mala y la buena traducción. Y, finalmente, Jorge Luis Borges descubre el misterio al afirmar que cada traducción es un borrador nuevo de la obra anterior. La conclusión podría ser de Goethe: sólo la gran poesía es traducible. O a la inversa, la gran poesía no puede traducirse.

M.V.

¿**Q**ué es traducir? ¿Un oficio, un azar, un acto de traición, una escritura de robot? Perplejidad. Ninguna definición de tan incómodo e imposible papel, satisface ni a incautos, ni a precavidos.

Cada generación traduce de nuevo, y de nuevo, incansablemente, aportando sombrías o risueñas demistificaciones. El texto llevado a contrapelo, se alborota, se aquieta, se enfurece y regresa siempre, lleno de otro con-texto. No hay, pues, tal Torre de Babel, sino una lengua propia, lalengua, así, pegado, con sus significados y significantes. El traductor tiene que conocer la suya, limpia y severamente, abordarla como a prostituta huidiza, sacarle lalengua frente a un espejo y, finalmente, obligarla a decir la gran poesía con otra lengua.

Traductores, somos todos. Traducimos o nos traducen, ello depende de nuestra fuerza o de nuestra debilidad. Cuando Lacan juega de manera gozosa con las palabras, y las pone a saltar con resortes de caja sorpresa, traduce. Cuando Borges hace que ocurra en español lo que ha ocurrido en inglés, y ejercita el modesto misterio, traduce. Y cuando escuchamos un capítulo de Dallas, en uno de sus múltiples doblajes, estamos siendo traducidos. Así de simple. Y ni tan simple.

No es lo mismo decir J'aime le fromage que Yo amo el queso. Alcanza lo surreal convertir una vuelta a la manzana en un tour a la pomme. Y es de ingenuos pensar que I Want significa Yo quiero, cuando en realidad es Yo carezco. Sólo en apariencia puede parecer incomprensible el je persevère y el je pére-severe de Lacan. Y, definitivamente, el francés empastela el inconsciente cuando hace el melancólico juego del ca-lembour: ce n'est pas la même chose les populations laborieuses du cap que les copulations laborieuses du pape.

Si aceptamos que primero fue la traducción y luego el original (léase Antiguo Testamento), debemos admitir que toda civilización depende de sus traducciones. Dependemos, atados de pies y manos y lengua, de esa figura imposible que es el traductor. Enemigo peligroso, si lo hace mal. Cómplice de alto vuelo, si lo hace bien.

De una edición del *Libro de horas*. Leipzig, 1918.

He aquí dos traductores frente a frente, sumergidos en un diálogo de espejos. Julieta Fombona de Sucre es una excepcional cómplice de Silvia Plath, de Roland Barthes y de Yeats. Su sueño intimida: quiere traducir a Marcel Proust de punta a punta. Pero su escritura, que suena a guijarro bajo la lengua, hace posible creer en todo sueño. Juan Luis Delmont-Mauri tiene en sus manos Memorabilia, una colección de Monte Avila para la traducción de textos escogidos y preciosos. Juntos, están compartiendo la-lengua de Jacques Lacan. Traducen lo que muchos estiman intraducible: los seminarios que el maestro dictó durante treinta años. Proeza que, según ellos, no lo es. De hecho, ningún traductor serio reconoce hacer buenas traducciones. Forma parte del imposible. De todos modos, estas traducciones son las oficialmente aceptadas. ¿Cien puntos para el país? ¡Ridículo!, responden

al unísono: el país no necesita calificaciones. Está lleno de excelencias. El problema es que los venezolanos, y el propio estado, pensamos en términos negativos.

Julieta y Juan Luis aceptaron hablar, ser grabados, sin importarles mucho la presencia de una tercera lengua. Corrieron el riesgo de ser traducidos. Y esto fue lo que ocurrió.

¿TRADUCTOR TRAIDOR?

Julieta. Uno de los problemas del traductor, es un problema de distancias. Cada lengua tiene una manera distinta de organizar el mundo. Y además, todo es un contexto. Hay que establecer la distancia que habrá entre el texto que llevas al español, y el inglés, por ejemplo. ¿Lo vas a poner completamente en español, es decir, parecerá que fue escrito en español? Si es así, no eres fiel al texto, porque no fue escrito en español. Si Lacan utiliza por ejemplo un refrán, puedes encontrar el equivalente, pero el refrán de Lacan puede estarse refiriendo a Rabelais o a La Fontaine. Encuentras un equivalente y es la voz de Sancho la que vas a oír, en la traducción al español. Yo diría que hay que encontrar un equilibrio entre una semántica y una semiótica. La semántica es el sentido: ¿qué dice este señor en inglés? y yo lo digo en español. Pero, ¿cómo lo dice? ¿cómo se hace el sentido en inglés? Allí está el problema. Y en la poesía es particularmente difícil. Nabokov, dice por ejemplo que todo traductor de poesía es un ser fraudulento. La poesía no se puede traducir, pero de hecho se traduce, porque si no, no conoceríamos a Hölderlin, ni a Goethe. Hay un imposible, pero hay una cosa práctica: también se traduce poesía.

Juan Luis. Goethe decía que sólo la gran poesía se puede traducir. Y como lo señala Borges, se dice exactamente lo contrario: la gran poesía no se puede traducir. Ambas cosas son verdades. Todos estamos de acuerdo en que en el Antiguo Testamento, en los evangelios, hay una gran poesía. Y muy pocos de nosotros habla el hebreo o el griego.

Julieta. Borges también dice que en la traducción está planteado el modesto misterio. Es verdad; dentro de una misma lengua uno traduce. ¿Qué es el diccionario? Traducir

from "Civilization rests on translation," which appeared in the magazine Criticarte *(December, 1985)*

TRADUCIR ES, SOBRE TODO, IDENTIFICARSE CON EL AUTOR

M.V.

Francisco Rivera ha sentido lo que él llama "el vértigo de las lenguas". Desde el italiano de las Estancias de Policiano, hasta el griego de los poemas de Cavafy, el crítico y ensayista conoce a fondo la dificultad de convertir en un texto poético real, aquel que se trae al español desde una lengua desconocida. Piensa que hoy, debido a la masiva comercialización del libro, el traductor es un ser explotado por la sociedad de consumo. ¿Traductor-traidor? Un criterio extremo, ya que Francisco Rivera sólo acepta hablar de traición cuando no se consigue un auténtico equivalente de traducción. Y siempre lo hay: basta saberlo buscar

e Francisco Rivera hay poco que decir. Y mucho que leer. Es uno de los ensayistas venezolanos más densos, más agudos y más críticos. Su firma aparece regularmente en Eco de Bogotá y Vuelta de México, para nombrar solamente dos revistas de indiscutible prestigio. En la Universidad de Berkeley, donde permaneció nueve años (1954-1963) sufrió varios vértigos: el budismo zen y la contracultura de Theodore Roszak, entre ellos, pero sobre todo uno, intenso, apasionado, absorbente, que lo mantiene todavía en constante éxtasis, la traducción.

os textos traducidos por Francisco Rivera del inglés y del francés, pasan de quince. Citemos La escritura y la experiencia de los límites de Philippe Solers y Razones de la nueva crítica de Serge Doubrovsky. Pero no hay duda: Cien poemas de Cavafy, traídos al español directamente del griego, es su obra maestra (palabra que lo incomoda). El propio Octavio Paz, ha dicho que es ésta la mejor traducción al español del gran poeta griego.

rancisco Rivera no rehuyó la participación en este dossier sobre el noble oficio del traductor. En esta breve entrevista, intentó detener el vértigo que le produce el traducir, aunque permaneció fiel a lo que escribió una vez en un ensayo sobre Cavafy y Pessoa: las traducciones no se terminan nunca.

12

ADMIRAR ES COMPARTIR

entro de su larga experiencia como traductor, ¿qué tipos de textos prefiere traducir?

—Hay dos tipos de traducciones. La traducción en prosa, ya sea de crítica literaria o de antropología o de sociología, etc. Hay que hacerla con cuidado, pero no es lo mismo que la traducción de un poema o de una serie de poemas, es decir, una traducción literaria importante. Considero que la que más ha exigido de mí, ha sido la traducción de poesía. Cuando uno admira un texto poético, desea compartirlo con otra persona. Y si ese texto está en otra lengua, ¿cómo compartirlo? Traduciéndolo.

—¿Cómo definir la tarea de un traductor?

—El traductor tiene que conocer bastante, lo mejor posible, la lengua del original. Y mejor aún, su propia lengua, para que ese texto dicho en una lengua desconocida, extranjera, pase a convertirse en un texto poético real, en la lengua de uno. Es una tarea que muchas personas hacen, sin tener conciencia de ello. Hace poco leí una traducción de unos poemas de Ezra Pound y me atrevo a decir que la persona que la hizo, no sabe inglés. Es como un torero espontáneo que se tira al ruedo, quizá por entusiasmo. Sé que el entusiasmo es un aspecto muy importante de esto, pero hay que tomar en cuenta el otro aspecto: estudiar, darle vuelta al texto, dominar la gramática de la lengua del poeta.

—Pero pareciera que por muchos esfuerzos que haga, un traductor siempre es un traidor...

—Claro, traduttore-traditore. El problema es que hay un texto original que tratas de convertir en un texto bello, poético, en tu propia lengua. Pero cada lengua tiene sus peculiaridades lingüísticas. Imagínate si tuviera que traducir del español al inglés, un poema que estuviera basado en la diferencia entre el verbo ser y estar. Sería un problema, porque ni el inglés, ni el francés, tienen dos verbos, uno para ser y otro para estar. Tendría que darle un giro distinto para traducirlo. Esos son los problemas que se encuentran en la traducción, pero particularmente en la poesía. Creo que se traiciona el texto, sólo cuando no se consigue un auténtico equivalente de traducción.

UN EQUIVALENTE PERFECTO

eer a Crimen y Castigo como si hubiera sido escrito en español, ¿no es una forma de traición al texto original?

—Hay una teoría según la cual, cuando uno lee una traducción, debe tener la sensación que, originalmente, fue escrito en esa lengua. Pero hay una teoría, apoyada nada menos que por Ortega y Gasset en su ensayo sobre la traducción, que sostiene todo lo contrario: el traductor debe dar la idea que el texto ha sido traducido y que hubo dificultades para traducirlo. Después de todo, Ortega y Gasset no era un experto en traducción, ni en lingüística, sino un gran filósofo. Creo que la mayoría de los grandes traductores y lingüistas actuales me darían la razón: hay que lograr un texto bello, correcto, que sea el equivalente perfecto de la lengua original...

—¿Cuál es a su juicio el nivel y la calidad de las traducciones que, en su mayoría, nos llegan de España?

—En España siempre ha habido excelentes traductores. Lo que pasa es que el nivel de la traducción al español ha bajado muchísimo, a causa de la comercialización del libro. En los años veinte y treinta, había muy buenos traductores, tanto en España como en Latinoamérica. Podría citar, entre otros, a Enrique Díaz Canedo y Alfonso Reyes. Era gente que traducía por amor a la literatura, sin importarle la remuneración económica. Actualmente, el traductor es un ser explotado por la sociedad de consumo, a quien se le

Miyó Vestrini on Translation

What is translation? A job, a chance procedure, an act of treason, a robotic task? Confusion. No definition of such a clumsy and impossible undertaking can satisfy either the wary or unwary.

Each generation translates again and again, tirelessly bringing serious or joyful demystification. The text takes it all, is disturbed, is still, rages and always comes back, now full of another text. There is, therefore, no Tower of Babel, but a language of its own, *lalangue*, thus stuck with its meanings and signifiers. The translator must know their own language, cleanly and severely, approach it like a fugitive prostitute, take its tongue in front of a mirror and, finally, force it to say great poetry from another language. . . .

If we accept that the translation was first and the original came after (read The Old Testament), we must admit that all of civilization depends on translation. We depend, with bound feet, hands and tongue, on that impossible figure of the translator. Dangerous enemy, if they do evil. The best accomplice, if they do well.

for La Negra

Introduction

I.

Grenade in Mouth: Some Poems of Miyó Vestrini is the most ambitious translation of Miyó Vestrini's poetry to date and the first full-length collection of her work available in English. Drawing from three decades (1960s-90s), *Grenade in Mouth* presents a comprehensive look at Vestrini's poetry, including both her best-known poems and previously unpublished work from the posthumously collected *Es una buena máquina* (*It's a good machine*; Letra Muerta).

The first section of *Grenade in Mouth*, selected from Vestrini's published volumes, spans Vestrini's career and demonstrates why hers is a major voice of the vanguard of Venezuelan Poetry. A member of the experimental literary groups Apocalipsis (Apocalypse), 40 Grados Bajo la Sombra (40 Degrees in the Shade), Sardio (Sardius), La Republica del Este (The Republic of the East), and El Techo de La Ballena (The Ceiling of the Whale), she wrote alongside Victor Valera Mora, Margara Russotto, and others of the Generación de Los 60s (The Generation of the 60s). As Vestrini challenged poetic form, she also challenged social convention. An uncompromising woman intellectual in a milieu dominated by men, Vestrini soon carried great influence in Venezuela and beyond.

The second section of this book, 2015's *Es una buena máquina* gathers fragments and poems from her archives. Edited by Vestrini scholar Faride Mereb, *Es una buena máquina* samples from the author's uncollected magazine publications, journals, and unpublished manuscripts. These texts expand and contract with the exhaustions of life and poetry and by doing so, create a sensitive portrait of a writer in process.

Miyó Vestrini was born in France, 1938, and given the name Marie-Jose Fauvelle Ripert. When she was nine, fluent in French and already reading the great poets in Italian, she emigrated to Venezuela with her mother, sister, and her stepfather, whose last name she took as her own. She was a rebellious child, and at eighteen, she joined Apocalipsis, the only woman to do so in the then male-dominated scene of the Venezuelan literary avant-garde. She soon became a dedicated and prize-winning journalist, directing the arts section of the newspaper *El Nacional* and writing columns in *Diario de Caracas*, *El Universal*, *La República*, *El cohete*, and others for many years. She published three books of poetry in her lifetime: 1971's *Las historias de Giovanna* (*The Stories of Giovanna*), 1975's *El invierno próximo* (Next Winter), and *Pocas virtudes* (Little Virtues), published in 1986. Vestrini died by suicide on November 29, 1991, leaving behind two collections: a book of poems, *Valiente Ciudadano* (Brave Citizen) and a book of stories, *Órdenes al corazón* (Orders to the Heart).

Grenade in Mouth is another book of Miyó Vestrini's: an imagined one. It is a work that remains eternally unwritten and unread. Bequeathed into being in her poem "Last Will and Testament," it is a legacy she leaves behind for her best friend Elisa Maggi (*La Negra*). This imaginary book takes its place in that will among a sad feeling and a small pleasure—Vestrini also wills La Negra her loneliness and her Ismael Rivera records—and in its title, it suggest the power of Vestrini's words to destroy both others and herself. *Grenade in Mouth* is more, however, than a book willed into being inside the magic territory of a poem, it is a phrase that shows up a second time in the poem "Brave Citizen." That poem—arguably one of Vestrini's best—dares God to find a death too vile or violent for its death-loving narrator. Teasing and flirting with God, too, she asks him for more than death: what she seeks is clarity:

> Allow me, lord
> to see me as I am:
> > rifle in hand
> > grenade in mouth
> > gutting the people I love.

We have called this book *Grenade in Mouth* not to presume that we have made the book Vestrini wanted—that version of *Grenade in Mouth* must be allowed to live in perfection inside the eternal desires of a poem—but because there is, as Vestrini must have known, no more apt descriptor of her work. This is a book that comes with a warning label. Readers must be careful. In the work of Vestrini, there is no casual or harmless reading.

Vestrini knew, of course, as she took her own life, that she would not live to make a book called *Grenade in Mouth*. It is with Elisa Maggi's permission and assistance that we have been able to make—if not a book that Vestrini herself imagined—a book that at least attempts to fill in the blank of her legacy, and it is with great pleasure that we are able to dedicate this other form of *Grenade in Mouth* to her.

II.

Critics have called Miyó Vestrini the poet of militant death. It is also said of her that her entire life was lived in service of its end. Vestrini is known, too, as the Sylvia Plath of Venezuela, but if she joins Plath as a confessional poet, what she is confessing is not a set of personal problems: it is a fatal disappointment with the world at large. Her work is less a self-exposure than a set of incantations. These poems are spells for a death that might live eternally, for what Vestrini offers readers is a fundamental paradox: how to create, through writing, an enduring extinction. Her poems are not soft or brooding laments. They are bricks hurled at empires, ex-lovers, and any saccharine-laced lie that parades itself as the only available truth.

In Vestrini's poetry, no form of tenderness is left unprosecuted. Her poetry is unafraid to spit at beauty and swaddle death in its arms. Maternal love is tossed out as unsentimentally as a child's soiled diaper ("turn eighteen / and snort all the coke you want / and puke on your mother's china'"). Romantic love is the precinct of rats. The love of a poet for poetry isn't let off easily either: its gendered absurdities are exposed ("[poets] write two lines and ejaculate. Alone'""), its false heroics dismantled. Even friendship is not spared, as in her elegy to her old friend Victor Valera Mora, who she lovingly mocks and chastises in death ("he died like an idiot / of a heart attack treated with chamomile tea'"""").

The love of life itself is the love met with Vestrini's fiercest resistance. When joy enters her poetry, it is always as an intruder breaking into an apartment not to burglarize but to try, against the tenant's will, to install some nice furniture. As Vestrini writes in "One Day of the Week I":

> if you choose
> you live.
> And if you live
> you enjoy.
> But joy is the horrific part of the dream

---

* "Caress"
** "The Smell"
**** "Chamomile Tea"

Joy attaches Vestrini regretfully, via life's available pleasures—sex, tortellini, a good song—to the existence her poems are always boasting she would rather do without. "I'll chose death," she writes, "but you could not have expected the leg of lamb to melt in your mouth."[****] Attended to with the zeal only available to one who would prefer to despise it, any pleasure appearing in Vestrini's poetry is the granular kind, slipped into the poems despite Vestrini's vigilance against it. It is pleasure, not fear, that is always throwing Vestrini off the path toward her end.

Miyó Vestrini was, even at her most morbid, clearly hilarious, too—the only kangaroo among the corpses, perhaps—and it is this humor that gives her poems a distinct charm. Accusing God, for example, as she does in the poem "Brave Citizen," of having a predilection for hot dogs, is typical Vestrini. Surprise becomes its own structure. A poem begging for death becomes, despite itself, one so funny its unintended side effect is a new will to live. Sufficiency, as a form of poetic organization, also reigns. Her mastery is often in giving the reader only just enough—a grease stain on the sheet, a breathtaking final line, a disorienting word in a list. In her poems, universes unfold in a wink, and a hint is as heavy as all the world. Vestrini does not let the reader fill in the blanks of her poems with boiler-plate lyricism: instead, having never omitted at least one unpoetic element—digestion, genitalia, cauliflower casserole, and peeling paint—from any of them, her poems keep even the white space around her words gritty.

There is, however, one love that Vestrini's poetry is helpless against: the love of death. The thanatophilia of these poems is erotic, unashamed, and indulged in with sometimes gleeful candor. If there is one thing about life to love without reservation, posits her work, it is that life is allowed the mercy of an end. Her writing about death, we believe, must be read on its own terms. Vestrini's poems seek to restore death and a desire for it as the concern of poetry, not therapy. Her work contains regular, explicit challenges to the institutions of mental health: "I find all my friends treated by psychoanalysts have become totally sad totally idiotic."[*****] It refuses the circumscriptions of "health" or "unhealth" that by the second half of the twentieth century, had come to domesticate death and particularly any desire for it. Instead, she is a stubborn acolyte of death as

---

[****] "One Day of the Week I"
[*****] "XII (Next Winter)"

20

it is found in the wilds—death as seen from among the elements, not from the therapist's couch.

That said, these are poems, not simply arguments, and it is obvious to us, too, that in existing in the near-perpetuity of print, these poems as poems curb and challenge the sentiments contained within. A self-preserving urge is in dialectical relation with the need to write oneself into oblivion. The very things that fill the poems with life are held up as evidence of death's necessity, and death's necessity is argued in its enduring form, to always be read by the living, and by extension, life. Death and poetry are always co-mingling among a scene of small pleasures and terrible feelings, but they are doing so for those who live, who are always also those who die. *Grenade in Mouth* is thus a document of an ardent wish to have one's death last indeterminably. In Vestrini's work, it is death, and not the foolish, flawed poet who sings of it, that is made immortal, or as she wrote in the poem *Beatriz*:

> Writing is not important, she wrote,
> and signed her name in small print,
> believing it apocryphal.

III.

Guillermo Parra, who has worked tirelessly and generously to bring Venezuelan poetry to Anglophone readers, first introduced us to the work of Miyó Vestrini, and it is only with his encouragement that we began to translate at all. He passed on to us a PDF of her collected poems, and as we began to translate—at first, strictly for our own use—one poem made us greedy for the next, in the way of enthusiastic readers, mostly, who can't wait to turn the page of the book. So we felt, too, about each line and its turn, each turn of phrase, too, excited to see what could happen next, what Vestrini would be unafraid to write. Vestrini's work began to take hold of us, creating such an urgency that we often felt as if we were in a translation emergency, needing to read something that we had only begun to reveal ourselves.

Without Faride Mereb, this book could not exist. Faride came to us with a vision for the first-ever English language book of Vestrini's work and as our discussions about the necessity of such a collection took off, our project evolved from the translation of her press Letra Muerta's beautifully designed and edited

Es una buena máquina into something more comprehensive. Faride was with us at every step of the way and it is only with her careful, rigorous eye and deep knowledge of Vestrini's work that these translations, that came from and for love and necessity, finally began to take a shape that could be shared beyond a living room in Kansas City. She has left a deep mark on these poems and we must credit her, too, with the brilliant idea for the title.

Sometimes it felt like by translating Vestrini's poems to English, we were attempting to use euphemisms to bandage bullet wounds. The English language's inadequacies when it comes to the vocabulary of feeling is a notorious problem for translators of Spanish poetry, and English also often lacks the capacity to pierce, pry, and sometimes assault in the way that Spanish can. Instead, we were left with our own language's worn out words, often puzzled at how to express Vestrini's ferocity without betraying it into cliché and how to express her poetry's whimsy without betraying it into error. Vestrini herself, however, well understood the difficulty of the translator's task, that "clumsy and impossible undertaking," and it was her courage in the face of her writing that continued to give us ours in translating not just Spanish into English, but poems into poems. In truth, Vestrini's poems are of the durable kind that forgive the crude hand of the translators at work on them. As Vestrini wrote in her own note on translation, "The text takes it all, is disturbed, is still, rages and always comes back, now full of another text." No matter how vast our inadequacies, they pale in comparison to her gifts. Vestrini's voice is so unmistakably her own that it would rise up without equivocation in any language, we think, and say what it must despite the bumbling efforts of any translators who have dared to offer themselves as its instrument. "All of civilization," she wrote, "depends on translation."

There is something else we must say, too. To translate Miyó Vestrini is like letting a deadly current pass through one's body and hoping not to get hurt. To read Miyó Vestrini is much the same, and any introduction to her work must end with a warning: of course this is dangerous territory. Of course you might feel some damage. Of course you must stay grounded, keep your feet on the floor. You must be careful, but if you are, you will feel the charge of her work without falling prey to its dangers. We believe that anyone lucky enough to read this work can be electrified into their senses. We hope you will find in Miyó Vestrini's deadly energy a resurrectional one.

—Anne Boyer and Cassandra Gillig

You Would Not Catch Me Alive

SIMPLE AS THAT

To walk on 42nd Street in New York City
or to blow on my fingers burning from chestnuts
on the corner of the Via Della Croce
or to be resplendent in the hustle of airports,
                              what would be the difference?

Of all skies, I live under the most common
the sky of the starving ones
planted above my head
with no motion beyond night and day.
Each day
I tell myself:
          you have to settle for these places
                              to return to them
because there, sometime,
                    you will have to die.

But the seasons and the plants persist,
the vulnerable rivers,
the tempests of passing trains,
the riddle of imprecise hours,
the fireball that crosses the edge of the window,
the exterminating angel dancing on the ceiling.

Get out of my life
                    they say,
as if life were that simple.

Simple as that.

The mirror turns soft under my fingers
                              begins to fill the house.

Grows from wall to wall
in the vertigo of my body
                    vertigo of meadows and soft light.

Astonishment returns.
Now I know:
Only women with beautiful eyes
do not age.

Only men with restless dreams
sing when they rise.

If I had known all this
                    you would not catch me alive.

ONE DAY OF THE WEEK I

When you were born
in 1938,
Cesar Vallejo was dying.
When your little head,
your navel,
your virgin cunt,
entered the world
from between the beautiful legs of your mother,
they were lowering the poet into a hole.
They covered it up with dirt
and you,
you were covered by memory.
You could not choose.
Because if you choose
you live.
And if you live
you enjoy.
But joy is the horrific part of the dream:
sleep will be forever.
There will be the smell of fried peppers,
thundering voices in the bar.
It will be a day of the week,
when furniture changes places in the night
and in the mornings,
the women will talk to themselves.
Your nose will be congested and the right eyebrow
will fall more than the left.
The flattened hips,
the bad haircut and the body lost
in any slip that hides the fat in your waist.
If you had sad lunatics for grandparents,
it will be reflected in the report
of a responsible official.
They will cross your arms over your chest
and this is fatal,

because you can not
use Afrin
to breathe better.
It was fake that your hugs were convulsive
and your furies unpredictable.
Fake, the glass you still steam with your burps.
Fake, your nipples, your red freckles.
Last night you decided:
if I cannot sleep,
I'll choose death.
But you could not have expected the leg of lamb to melt in your mouth,
soft,
milky,
on your tongue.
You could only say:
two childbirths,
ten abortions,
no orgasms.
You took a long sip of wine.
Vallejo also sought a leg of lamb
in the menu of La Coupole.
All watched his stupid eyes,
while he could only think about the quiet ears of Beethoven.
He had asked his companion:
Why do you not love me anymore?
What did I do?
Where did I fail?
The sausage in the casserole left grease stains on his shirt.
Like you,
he felt compassion tired his body
and tried to guess who would be born on this night,
while trying to fall asleep.
Dying
requires time and patience.

ONE DAY OF THE WEEK II

Shutting his eyelids to block the light of noon
was never a problem for Modigliani.
The truth is always waiting for us
at the bottom of the bottle,
he warned,
long before lengthening the necks of his women.
It is degrading to eat in bed,
but I do
at the risk of losing the company of El Flaco.
The disheveled bed,
the book of Levi-Strauss and Didier,
the crumpled paper napkin,
how many years spent wandering around here?
Belly down to watch television,
face up to be loved,
elbows folded for sleep.
Life does not form part of the universe's great laws:
I am a solitary fate
in this space of twilight and rituals.
I now escape the perspective of those who board a bus
or piss behind a tree.
Chimpanzee eating a turkey and mustard sandwich.
It's April and myopic eyes blink
in delicious successive messages:
postmodernism, cliques, preps, gays, the borderline.
Living cells that undress me and recount my memory.
I touch my little thing, tidy with so much iodine soap
washed
and re-washed thoroughly.
An island that smells of iodine.
Little thing conducive to the entry of fungi, herpes, bacteria, bugs, foams,
plastics, copper and rubber.
Come here, brat.
El Flaco caresses me with a fatherly hand:
don't berate your little thing,

she is much more useful than art.
Once again, that child playing violin on the next floor.
I seem to see him—chubby, overbite,
smelling of polyps and inflamed tonsils,
a huge callus on the chin.
There he goes again with the scale,
nasally,
raspy,
sluggish.
Fuck, screams the Spaniard from the fifth floor.
My mother told me,
tu me fais grincer les dents,
nothing to do with the
tu me tue, tu me fais du bien,
of Hiroshima Mon Amour.
Anyway, long before this
Shakespeare had determined
that every man ends up killing what he loves.
The folds of the sheet hurt my back
as he read the horoscope out loud this morning.
Clean and full refrigerator.
The beer can with its frosted edges
and ham wrapped in aluminum foil.
A question of values:
walkman, gastronomy, zen, cool, humanism,
nobody will be defrauded by manipulation.
I choose the beer
and run back to bed.
I wonder if human rights really
are an ideology.
Fernando, the only alcoholic bartender who hasn't retired,
speaks in rhymes:
the night is dark
and I don't have my heart.
As I understand it, he's one of the few left who
thinks human rights are morals.

I fluff the pillow,
I suck my thumb,
and I hope that El Flaco comes.
There are days like this.

THE CALL

When I asked him why he had not called
he explained to me that he had been buried alive
and that he did not have a phone.
In his thin chicken lips
there is
or was not
any daring.
Everything was strictly legal.
Is it because you do not believe in God?
If it wasn't easy,
you wouldn't try to do it.
Significance,
signifying,
significantly,
sign.
I went to the balcony
and looked at the park,
irritating brotherhood of screaming children
and calibrated birds.
Heard the remote control changing channels,
no sound.
I felt at my back
his desire to put on his pants
and leave.
I went to the kitchen to peel potatoes.

THE SORROW

I folded his shirts with care
and emptied the nightstand drawer.
Given my sorrow's size,
I read Marguerite Duras,
hostile and saccharine Marguerite Duras,
who is knitting a shawl for her love.
On the fifth day
I opened the curtains.
Light fell on the grease-stained bedspread,
the apartment full of trash,
the door frame peeling.
So much pain
from such ugly things.
I looked once more at his rat face
and threw all the trash in the garbage chute.
The neighbor
alarmed by how much I'd thrown away,
asked if I was doing all right.
It hurts, I told her.
In my mailbox, an anonymous note:
"One who has love
takes care
takes care
and does not clog the drain of the community."*

---

* The first part of this note references the song "Salud, Dinero y Amor" by Gigliola Cinquetti.

LITTLE THING, IN TRUTH

It does not take long so I should tell you:
> I tremble when I talk of it.
> Little thing,
>> in truth.

GRATED CARROT

The first suicide is unique.
They always ask you if it was an accident
or a sincere proposition of death.
They shove a tube up your nose,
hard,
so it hurts
and you learn to not disturb the neighbors.
When you begin to explain that
death-actually-seemed-like-the-only-way-out
or that you did it
to-fuck-up-your-husband-and-your-family
they have all turned their backs
and are watching the transparent tube
retrieving the parade of your last supper.
Betting on whether its noodles or fried rice.
The doctor on duty coldly tells them:
it's grated carrot.
"Disgusting," says the nurse with big lips.
They disposed of me furiously,
because no one won the bet.
The saline dispersed quickly
and ten minutes later,
I was back at my house.
No space to mourn
nor time to feel cold and tremble.
People are unconcerned with death that comes from loving too much.
Child's play,
they say,
as if children killed themselves every day.
I looked in Hammett for this exact page:
never tell a word about your life
in any book,
if you can help it.

XII (from *Next Winter*)

for Luis Camilo

I get up
I do not get up
They hate me
I tie my tubes
I hit a motorcyclist with malice aforethought
I surrender to the Oedipus complex
I wander
I carefully study the differences between dysrhythmia -
psychosis - schizophrenia - neurosis - depression - syndrome - panic
and I'm pissed
left alone in the house when everyone is asleep
I buy a magazine that costs six dollars
they steal my best friend's purse
they grab me
I love my friend
I push him
I murder him
I remember the umbrella from Amsterdam
and the rain
and the angry gesture
I dedicate myself to drinking to prevent heart attacks
I chew my food fifty times
and I'm bored
and I'm bored
losing weight
gaining weight
losing weight
I give in
I don't give in
I sit still and cry
someone takes me in his arms
and tells me, "Be calm I'm here"
I stop crying
I hear the wind that blows near the sea, only near the sea

I accept that flying cockroaches exist
I find that all my friends treated by psychoanalysts have become
totally sad totally idiotic
they read my I Ching and predict I'll have a long life
life of shit, I say
I join the bandwagon
I throw myself under the bandwagon
I understand for a single trip how much gas is in the tank
they tell me to turn off the light
I turn it off
they ask me, "You done yet?"
I play stupid
I plead for peace
they fuck me up
I fall asleep up against the bar
I hear the Spaniard's voice whenever he shits on god*
someone cries beside me again
they hit me
they hit me hard
there's a full moon
I race down the mountain road
I do the math
it doesn't add up
my chest hurts,
the day is done,
the Red wins
rien ne va plus

---

* In Spanish, an impossibly good phrase: me cago en diez. Diez (ten) being a substitute for Dios (god). A softer way of saying you'll shit on god.

CARESS

Half of what happens to my son
will be my fault.
Good.
She says like that,
covered with necklaces and moles,
twenty-four hours after I sent you to Paris
to learn the language
and know what it was like to be away from home.
It comes to me
your messy teenage face,
as if raised to a teacher eager to straighten up
this little man with old money.
You have to be strong,
they tell you:
only then will you have the right
to turn eighteen
and snort all the coke you want.
And puke on your mother's china
at the dinner held
to celebrate your return.
For now,
you shake from cold in the dorm of the greats
and touch the pendant that your girlfriend gave you
at the airport.
I have not finished with you yet, said the note,
I'd prefer others do.
Signed:
Mama loves you.
They kicked you out of the gallery of mirrors
so you would not disrupt the design of the Dutch architecture.
Even before your arrival
she suffered from the baby blues
because,
oh, I moaned,
I'm not ready to be a mother.

Now it's you
who is not ready to be a son.
You hate what is right,
you hate what is wrong.
You are lost between Pere Lachaise
and Rue Delambre.
There aren't as many memories as you would like.
Already you play with immortality:
poor rat,
worthless in a bet,
you shout at bystanders as the sun sets.
You look at toilet paper
impregnated with your sad child's poo.
Of a bad boy
sent to Paris with a note around his neck:
minor traveling alone.

USE

What I do not use:
>the bus to El Silencio
>the transformer
>the Delft hen
>the book *Film 1962* by Vittorio Spinazzola
>Berrocal's detachable sculptures
>the egg timer
>the concierge's bell
>the hotel suggestion box
>the sixth speed of the blender
>pay stubs
>barf bags
>an Istanbul travel guide
>life insurance for the blind
>a criminal record
>the people's liberation
>and the words
>>to fold and unfold

THE STORY OF O

When you wake up
keep quiet
find ecstasy

Accept extravagance
cry for submission
ignore the arguments
be angry at all excesses of love

the water of graves will be in you
                           water of swamps and prayers
the unbearable will come later
when the wind makes waves in the pond
and you cannot see
               as you disappear under the earth

CLOUDS OVER THE CIRCUS

Carolina's morning starts at 11
the extravagant punctuality
of insomniacs.
This new type of waking requires small routines.
Cleaning her sleepy and mascara-stained lids,
until her eyes are enormous and isolated, bare
in the middle of a cover
white
and pasty.
Carolina remembers a star on the cheek of a girl
suspended on a trapeze.
Her smile brilliant in the darkness of the bathroom.
The skin becomes transparent again.
Matted and opaque hair flies solo.
Carlos contemplates it while hunched over in the leather chair,
lethargic,
profound.
Carolina has large fingers with stubby nails
and when she lifts her thin arms,
she shows her badly shaved armpits.
Today is friday,
sweet friday, she recalls.
It is not sweet friday,
it is Faulkner's tender thursday, he responds.
Carolina was an unplanned pregnancy
the result of copulating on sunday.
Her mother brought her outrage with regularity:
your father is a s-h-i-t, she spelled out.
The maid robs us,
the chauffeur is having sex with her,
the roast is burnt,
I don't have anything to wear.
Carolina falls asleep,
face under the blanket.
Still missing some steps

that would complete the routine.
The shower, the hairstyle, the dress to choose.
Leaders in Rome, in Leningrad, in Mexico.
A question: Who said that the revolution was in excess?
Trotsky, responded Carlos.
The stars and comets are not free,
who said that?
An actor named Gene Amoroso, in the film
Three Women.
Carolina eats a slice of cheese.
A slice of turkey.
A spoonful of honey.
Both stare, waiting for something for happen.
The old can do what they want,
it's not important to anyone.
Throw out what doesn't work.
Dripping of soup and salsa.
Spitting and burping.
Give me time, says Carlos.
After a huge silence, I am very patient with you,
says Carolina.
All right.
How does a fight between lovers start?
Putting clouds over the circus.
Talking over one another.
Being compassionate.
Eating capers.
Cut,
murmurs Carolina.
She gets up,
light,
in good humor.
Let's go out,
I don't want to lose my identity.
Carlos straightens the neck of his wretched shirt
and takes her to eat in a restaurant with no stars.

SCHEDULE

What did you do today?
> I read the newspaper and didn't recognize any friends.
> I defrosted my fridge so the beer would stay cool.
> I took a bubble bath.
> I dried my hair.
It doesn't seem like you did much.
> I do a lot and no one realizes.
> I can see myself in the bottom of the pots
> and in the kitchen floor.
But you didn't go out. You'd promised.
> I was at the stop.
> I raised my hand and no one pulled over.
Neither did you read the book I bought you.
> I didn't have time.
You never have time.
> Neither do you. And I don't bother you by asking
> "What did you do today?"
Think of how the hours pass in this house.
> They pass,
> I assure you,
> they pass.

LIZARDS

There are men
        who open the covers
                and enter.

Without fresh turmoil
without heat or melancholy
without casting a spell

        They are lizards.
             Banished.
                Miserable.

THE GOOD REASONS

I

As if there were still time for awkwardness,
and adolescence,
I think about Venice,
because of the blinds that go up and down
a sound like no other.
More than the nauseating rain,
I am shaken by things I remember,
shit things.
In the changing season,
when the mist retreats from north to south,
my relatives die in the distance
coagulated in a clay cup.
With nostalgia's grim privilege
I know for sure
that outside the big cities
nothing but the sea is bearable.

II

It's time to nourish myself with the afternoon
and to sing
like the rest of the world
I can't stop loving you
time to prevent against maternity bills
against those who toast to their generation
against the relief of not waiting for anyone
against this house,
where there is a daily risk of death
without even having read Ian Fleming.

III

Everything always started because of the tumult,
as if women born under the sign of Taurus
stopped being gentle after childhood.

I am of those who forget every year
of the same era.
Then I hear rain from the bed,
while the dead's feeble delirium
floats in the living room
amidst the rustling of papers and drawers,
among a jumble of sharp and severe days.
  And at the same time:
  —My story with you has ended
  Since you do not know of
  Manhattan, or the Via Dei Fiori
  Scuri, or the Hotel Primavera.

IV

Some still talk
of bad childhoods they never had,
of the mansion they were building on the outskirts of the city,
of the criminal implications of the commons,
of Elenora, the newborn,
of the dead,
of Marienbad,
of childbirth without pain,
of bankrupt families,
of loneliness,
of some woman they met in a bar,
of being exhausted.
  All this,
  with a lack of irreversible grace.

V

In the villages where we once lived,
the people are hard and melancholy,
as if nothing were in reach,
as if it were useless to put things in their places,
to give in before dying,
to have that mean and cold air
appropriate to euphoria.

I try in vain to make the spirits talk
from a messy and compassionate place.
Defeated in advance by their anger
they lose their sentimental habits forever.

VI

> There was a certain foul and ridiculous age:
> —if in Massachusetts, for example, someone
> raises his glass and urinates on the deserted meadow,
> no one should be there.

The ships were then
matters of public interest.

VII

To let oneself be comforted by childhood,
my best friend was a round, smelly girl,
she learned to fondle herself
breast and neck
as you now learn to have friends.
She calls me the birthgiver of a good death
and between the sea and the city, she says:

> ...the health of the people...

And her voice is lost in the night.
Behind her,
some dreadful anecdote.

VIII

One dies without having stopped thinking
in the house of friends,
where I now remember
with wordless pleasure
the wine of an Italian tavern.
In some untamed territory,
the wild knight of the roses
still has memory for all of us,
and for me,
the breathless memory of that longhand

in multiple languages,
beginning again to throb
dense and milky in the dark.

IX

It was useless to think
about who would close the eyes of these Europeans
rambunctious on a summer patio.
Families of three children,
faithful to a sweaty nap,
lost in some nightmare fog
and mining towns of the north,
waiting for a disaster,
of those that occur in Europe,
in the morning,
when it is Sunday evening here.

X

      The way I spend my time
      never makes me laugh.

XI

After cracking the parlor
wide open,
my father forced me to sit there,
and not speak
for any reason.
Grandfather,
coming from Dublin,
had died
while crossing the town square.
And the buzz was around all afternoon:
      ...oh delirium of well nourished children
      who are angry
and love the love of their mothers...

I thought I saw then
from the stock market's balcony
to resurrect those who lost it all.

BEATRIZ

With or without a dick,
there are things that cannot be done
when you start to sweat
or when the prostate hurts.
So Beatriz killed herself
at the age of fifty-three.
She did not want to participate in the grotesque ceremony
of eulogizing decadence.
She covered all the mirrors
and put satin sheets on the bed.
She was supposed to die there
neat and fragrant
ignoring the rat who bit her breath away
But she preferred the sofa
where she had made love the night before
with a professional party boy
rented for the occasion.
She left a list
of mistakes and successes.
Writing is not important, she wrote,
and signed her name in small print,
believing it apocryphal.

NO MORE

No more black Cardin dresses
stuffed with Cardenal Mendoza.
No more brats with rolling eyes
bony elbows
and awful silences.
No more signs turning people away.
No more invitations to worry about the day before.
No more patronage.
No more sunset tremor
without any allegation but its own.
No more dead to mourn from afar
because they died without you.
No more chubby gentle girls
pushed around by nuns.
No more limelight.
No more envy of those who are landing
right now
in San Francisco.
No more fear of astrology.
No more belief in curses
or scrying the candlelight
for the arrival of the lord.
No more asking for love and feeling miserable.
No more jerks on the payroll.
No more giving your all
no more
fucking
no more.

BRAVE CITIZEN

to María Inmaculada Barrios

Die in thought
every morning and you will not
be afraid to die.

—*The Hagakure Guide*

Give me, lord,
an angry death.
A death as offensive
as those I've offended.
A death that stands for the rains
of Santiago de Compostela,
a death that kills
all who have offended me.

Give me, lord,
a death from the elements,
one that stuns and petrifies.
Wastes snot and tears
pleading for mercy
and wishing death on anyone else.

Make sure, lord,
that the man with unknown skin
recognizes in me an animal of the olive groves.
Let your body weigh down mine
and sweeten
the entrance to the fire.

I swear I have seen it all.
The same guilt with which I was born,
the same fury.
Make sure, lord,

that I am listening to Vinicius de Moraes
and María Bethania
and promising that tomorrow,
Monday,
I will enroll in a course to learn Brazilian.

Let death come
when you find in me
some hidden intention of power
and when you know,
from your informants,
of my conspiracy to go down in history.
When they say, lord,
that I have exhausted all the resources of fatigue
without asking for clemency,
then, lord,
give it to me hard.
Make this knot on my forehead
from opening doors with headbutts
turn
red,
pounding,
painful.

Suppose, lord,
that you are the big-bang.
That no territory escapes your vigilance.
That hot dogs are the subject of your predilections.
That your desire for me is an obscene part
of your personality.
Then, lord,
Examine my bulging stomach
        for the spaghetti of Portofino
        for the *favadas* of Guernica
        for my mother's cauliflower casserole
        for the long drinks of beer and rum.

Observe, lord, the faces of my mirror in the mirror,

I, the astute pusillanimous
finger in the air
fanning the boring crowd.

You could come to the movies, lord.
We would see *Brazil*,
La vaquilla,
Partie de Campagne
Il Postino and *Gatsby*.
You would listen to me
trembling with laughter
and fear.

Allow me, lord,
to see me as I am:
       rifle in hand
       grenade in mouth
       gutting the people I love.

Lie with me at dawn, lord,
when my breath is a boulder
in the stream.

And you will see that nothing
       not even the milk of your psalms,
can give me a death that enrages me.

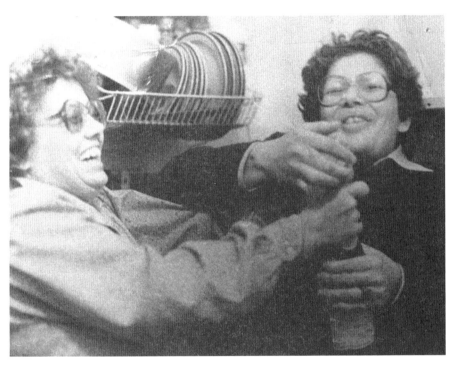

Vestrini and La Negra, circa 1970-75

LAST WILL AND TESTAMENT

They ask you
to whom will you leave your things when you die?
So I looked over my house
and its stuff.
There was nothing in it to give up,
but my rancid smell.
And the rat.
The rat that stayed hostile and silent,
waiting for it to occur.
Useless, to feed it
and soften its bed with blue soap.
I waited for it every night,
anxious to see how its long mustache
would stop hiding the sharp and predatory teeth.
It was there,
staring sneaky
and unspeaking as a sphinx,
hoping that my blood would run.
Futile waiting
death arrived inside
first, calm and definitive.
I wrote your name on the wall,
so the final sunburn,
at about ten am
drew a shadow in my will:
"The rat did not allow me to see the spring"
When dead,
I made the list.
Dinner at the best restaurant
for Ángeles and Carlos.
My books, my unpublished works for José Ignacio.
My dreams for Ibsen.
My credit card for Ybis.
My car for Alberto.
My double bed for Mario.

My memory for Salvador.
My loneliness for La Negra.
My Ismael Rivera records for La Negra.
My poems called "Grenade in Mouth" for La Negra.
My pain from adolescence and motherhood, for Pedro.
My ashes for Ernesto.
My laughter for Marina.
Last night,
I told Ángeles and Carlos
if I cannot sleep,
I will choose death.
The leg of lamb was so tasty
that they barely heard me.
I remember that on one corner of Chacao,
she put her arms around me and said,
next friday we will invite you.
Her hair cut short
and her happiness to have it that way
made me realize that she was not just Carlos' silenced mother.
I rested my cheek on her shoulder.
It was only seconds,
but I felt that as the scissors had cut through her mane,
something had changed.
Something that doesn't go by her name
now haunting the sleepless and drunken nights
in the neighborhood of the family.
To die deliberately,
requires time and patience.
You evoke the gratuitous death of a son,
a thing that never happened to you.
The loss of objects
and the silence of a devastated house,
didn't happen to you either.
The ferocious finger of an enemy pointing to you
as if without remorse.
It happens, but it's not mortal.
Two births,
ten abortions

and no orgasms.
One good reason.
The silence of your lover when you ask him,
Why don't you want me?
What did I do?
Where did I fail?
and then the tour of those spaces quiet
and empty,
with you bent over,
awkward.
Validating that there is neither soap for the wash
nor starch for ironing
and at best
those oranges are rotten.
Then you remember:
being on a terrace at 7 am,
overlooking the sea,
and someone saying to you,
this gives me a fear of heights
but I love you.
And then,
returning to the city
and to the mazucamba of a naked and joyful man.
You think again about what is deliberate.
It is not fate.
It is not vengeance.
It is one's hand
sweaty palm,
touching one's thigh.
Going back a little more
and recalling the uneasiness of your lover,
the shadowy stench
of your pleasure.
There is always a before
before dying.
Before,
I want to eat tortellinis in cream.
Or take a drink of Tanqueray.

Or be embraced with strong arms.
Or, as Caupolican says,
that they put me in the presence of Maiquetia,
the most beautiful city in this whole country.
No one
that I know
has deliberated on their own disappearance.

CHAMOMILE TEA

My friend,
El Chino,
once wrote about how women sit
and walk
after they've made love.
We never got to argue about it
because he died like an idiot
of a heart attack treated with chamomile tea.
Had we had the chance,
I'd have told him that the only thing good about making love
is men who ejaculate
without bitterness,
without dread.
And that after doing it,
no one wants to sit down
or walk.
I named an old palm tree
planted near the pool at my apartment after him.
Every time I take a drink
and I greet him,
he shakes his leaves,
a sign that he's furious.
He told me once:
life's a massive happiness
or a massive outrage.
I'm true to my childhood dreams.
I believe in what I do,
what my friends do,
and what everyone like me does.

Sometimes we stay up together
very late
talking about the worms that hound him
and the wicked heat he feels all day
in that aridity and sand.

He hasn't changed:
hungry,
dispossessed,
he can sit down and befriend Mallarmé.
Lautréamont joined us one night
and said El Chino was right:
poetry should be made by all.
And then the others came:
Rubén Darío leading Nicaragua,
Omar Khayyam with his parties,
Paul Éluard uniting lovers.
Together,
we dipped El Chino in the pool, under a full moon,
and he was content
like when he had a river,
some birds,
a kite.

Now he's worked up again,
because they bring him flowers
while he's trying to scare off cockroaches.
He wanted to be interred in Helsinki,
under eternal snow.
He went around the world,
passing through London where a woman waited for him,
and on his way back,
he drank chamomile tea.
He,
who loved the shadows so much,
could no longer stay up all night.
Lucid and very hypocritical,
he had a horrible fear of dying in bed.
I know
because he wrote me a note
that the line he liked most was David Cooper's:
a bed is the laboratory of love and dreams.

DIAGNOSIS

Let's see,
open your mouth.
Say aaaah.
Show me what your mother did when you were a girl.
Was that the secret?
Oral sex?
Manipulation?
Touch?
Manipulation?
Consider your uterus,
broad and outdated.
How many children passed through there?
The doctors told you
that nature awaited them.
But they just died.
And if they lived
some would have been morons
others more or less the same,
all premeditated out of loneliness.
You have problems with your teeth,
with the slow digestion of the indecisive,
with the crunch of the occipital bone.
You're just another patient.
Everyone would like to have been born in Kansas City
or in Amsterdam
or in Toronto.
Or at least
twenty years later.
Let me shake this ivory specimen,
verify the mixture's color.
Disgusting,
how bad you smell.

CONTEMPT OF DEATH

Contempt of death
              I'll try it

The witness has turned his back
The house has been demolished

So much silence for such a small pain

       Fuck up, you said? Always bad words with you
You're nonsense. You're playing with intemperance and if
you are tired of trying then nobody will relieve you of the shadow and the
pause. *Fuck up*, you said?

The hounds don't come:
                    they have always been there.

The whisper of the warning
             strains my throat

When I wake up
          another day
                devoured by night
I hear sirens firecrackers smells
and nothing that quenches my trembling

            Hi how's it going what's up what's
new what are you up to well nothing I don't know when will we
see each other call me come here don't stop doing it if you saw
how sad it is but it's not important tomorrow will be different
good last night don't talk about that remember what Salvador
said don't torment me have a drink you'll get over it
and what am I gonna say again to apologize it's always
going to be like this you have to understand don't stop see
you at one o'clock I'll be waiting

I hear myself cracking up
        debating
                smiling
                        breaking
                                moaning
And I never left a trace
other than these steps of infamy

DON'T COME BACK HERE ANYMORE

To hell with all this
and I lasted years without going to hell
it's why I've come to see her.

>   If you were feeling that depressed,
>   would you think of all this? Would you
>   have come to see me?

I'm just gonna say:
Talk to me, don't write this down

>   We'll see. Tell me how
>   you're feeling. I know that you're alone and don't
>   know what to do. Make an effort.

I like the room.
The sun trades places with
the twilight. I try not to clear
my throat. I keep still.
I think of a
ram with huge
horns, walking
on a Persian carpet.

>   You are full of it.
>   Understand?
>   Full of gross things. One after another.
>   Your mother, for example.
>   And your father. What's happened?

I would like to visit the house.
It's a house of a madam prim and
proper. I feel that I've
melted into my chair. It's the
moment when you bring flowers to

someone. Of drunkenness. Of
middle age.
I'm scared.

> You have to turn back. To live life
> like you've not really lived. It's a
> long journey. Very long. Take advantage
> now while you're at the edge of
> the cliff. Write, but only a couple of
> lines. Think.

Yes. That's it. I'll make love, but
only for a few minutes. I'll cry
just a few tears, nothing more. I'll yell, but
only when it's justified. I'll never be shrill.
The clock is ticking, poor thing. I'll try
not to forget your face
in order to recognize it
on the Society page.

> Tell me something important. One
> important moment, like the one that
> we're living right now. You want to be alone,
> to hide yourself away, right? Or maybe you want
> to die? You've had crazy ideas?

Who would touch
me when I'm dead?
Elias's *Deaths* smell
like dogs. I don't want it. When
some people die, we pour
one out. All that death
yet I'm crazy for thinking this way.

> Let's see. You're a girl.
> Ten years-old. You're not afraid of
> anything, not even bats.
> Your mother takes your arm.

67

Takes you for a walk in the village.
She speaks of demons and apparitions.
You resist the arm that
envelops all. Was it then that
you felt afraid?

People and demons. What could
a girl know about all that? I came to ask
for the hellworld of the disappeared.
And you return me to the city, to the light
that would lead me to gloom.
Before closing the door, she says to me:

Don't come back!

THE HOUR OF WHORES AND OBSTINATE DOGS

At this hour
no one knows what to do

      and it's always at this hour of whores and obstinate
dogs when I remember. Every day, lost in time, you
know, face in hands, knees to chin, the living picture
of pain in the heavy afternoon. Immobile in the
rubble, immune to disaster, it could not be
any other way.

And it's the same hour
            of the day
                  that comes every day
that fucks me up.

IN THE COURTYARD OF ANAÏS NIN

In the courtyard of Anaïs Nin
I waste my mortality

>ruined but stubborn, I fill the water glass for the sweat of dawn and
>straighten the quilt seeing little spiders frozen on the roof, always
>from the cold of the night before, always the same,

and from this courtyard, I remember especially the smell,
that meeting nobody took down,
because the day was very gray
and we feared
that people would wake with sadness.

And how unbelievable the courtyard.
The statue of the child with an unshakeable stare,
dashes of sky, rain and doves.
A traveler who lied to avoid his destination.
April's strange transients.
A murderer unaffected by the breeze.

>that used to say "don't be afraid," they are wooden
>noises of some neighbor's melancholy,
>of someone's ghost. And they used to follow prowlingly,
>watch and plot against the fog, almost abandoning
>their own time, but with no time
>to start something new.

In the courtyard of Anaïs Nin,
the bad days sometimes awaken

>awaken the water and the bells and the
>rigorous words and the blind fury of those
>kept alone and hit above the eyes and those
>who see you like nothing is happening. A whole
>squawking anger, roaring, uneasiness,

70

confusion, monotony, until the stillness
of death, when agitation renders you useless.

In the courtyard of Anaïs Nin,
drinks are sweet and demonic

    round and round

applaud my beloved,

    the most loved of the lunatics.

In the courtyard of Anaïs Nin
they don't accept strangers

    or those who come from choleric countries.

In the high ceiling, there will be time for your body and mine

    without talk about your bliss, about your
    jasmine mornings, your unbearable
    disasters. You will run under the fast pace
    of the clouds and you will join lock
    and key.

In the courtyard of Anaïs Nin,
when you sleep and you love me,
now is the day all the furies unite.

ONLY YOU WILL SPEAK, MY FRIEND

I have spoken of unhappiness
       hasty mornings
              bitter sun
                     meridians

I have spoken of indecision
       percale drunkenness
              livid mouths
                     palms up

I have spoken of insults
       hands on the table
              exit adolescence
                     belly of honey

I have spoken of the insolent
       laughter
              waste
                     bitterness

But in the hills
       others will speak of
              the ones lost of fate

Of the splendors
of the fervent and pure desires
of secret explosions in our mouths
of sweet body curvature awakening
              only you will speak
                   my friend.

OF LITANIES AND LITTLE VIRTUE

There are many
who will jump into battle
and hurt me
       to death

death of the grandest cities
and littlest virtues
adrift on seven continents
your dismal peace from last October
your elastic flesh sweet
              and choleric

choleric sand flung about Ostia
scuffing crystal globes in the shop windows
a lifeless eye
the other opened
         to the avenue
avenue where it arrives
            the water
water of all the days
approached
     my mouth
mouth sad with big words
hard language on the tongue like fresh cut wood
takes care
     of me
my crime
crime of long and deep nights
when the rain takes forever to fall
and everything makes me think
my father
my mother
the land
     poorly closed

73

closed by four criminals
                              no identities

identities, your name, mine
the others
                    the people

loved people
absent
present
                    gone

gone
like my aunt
with her red hair in Bordeaux
                    in the house
house of hard knocks
where you try not to cry over nothing
while, just above you,
countryside and its little monsters
celebrate daily
a greeting
a writing
                    a vilification
a vilification:
he who has written it among you may
throw the first
stone
stone from no place other than my dwelling
when tenacious arms taught me disaffection
the pawnshop
the uncertainty
                    the return
return from the last act
act of being so sad and so dead
like the solitudes of other
                              countries
countries where they did not let me

74

           go
go with amazement
for one or two
       words
words
wait
I will teach you
boleros or *saudades* or petulant melancholy
or boldness

boldness is
of bars
of beloved places
of finding the man of your life
of mistreating that which was
                 your mother
mother
once dead
there was neither loneliness
nor rigorous exercises
        to forget
forget that the miserable,
alien
      to love,
love

THE WALLS OF SPRING

I will not teach my child to work the land
nor to smell the tang of the earth
nor to sing hymns.
He will know that there are no crystal streams
no clean drinking water
His world will be hellish downpours
and dark plains.

Of cries and groans.
Of dry eyes and throats.
Of tortured bodies that no longer will be able to see or hear him.
He will know that it is not good to hear the voices of those who exalt the
color of the sky.

I'll take him to Hiroshima. To Seveso. To Dachau.
His skin will fall piece by piece in front of the horror
and he will listen with sorrow to the bird's song,

> the laughter of the soldiers
> the death squads
> the walls of spring.

He will have the memory that we never had
> and will believe in the violence
> of those who believe in nothing.

It's a Good Machine

THE TRIP

I'll tell you how I know what I am:

they say that I was conceived without sin
my cries were answered with other cries
people went on vacation and left me
gave away my New Year's clothes
disowned the shame when I was absent
I had no mourners for my trespasses
threw breadcrumbs at watery graves
placated my own desires
held the ground between myself and the penumbra
bought a dog and let it out
paid Cesar Vallejo to love me
passed without glory or pain beneath the Mirabeau Bridge
I don't have a single friend dead in the war
no one knows my name for sure
and yesterday
they betrayed me without asking permission

FALLEN WOMAN

Body of all imperfections
one night I spoke of you
apostrophes and laments
I held strong to its delirium
                caught you
and knew no more of you

THE WORLD

Wet from you
I escape to the roundabout
open myself to the walls of the city
like an ornamental corn

return full of laughter
and of cravings
as if this were really the chosen world
the chosen night
the moment of all plenitude

FROM HERE

Being alone
has become something so miserable
that I write
thinking for whom I write
It's about moving them in some way
when they're vain
the desire to set aside time
repeating
for years
I don't know what to do
I don't know what to do

THE FOG

What didn't happen then
when inflamed memory promised life and dreams
becomes a song of beggars
in the hot fog of midday

Misfortune offers possible mercies
but the vanquished have manias of their own

They return time and time again
speak of the Mediterranean when the war was in the Pacific
have no pity
have forgotten the premonitions

And memory becomes a lonely warning
for the few who still gather around the stirred up fire.

THE HOUSE

All have returned home
           except for you
They saw the blood in the gutter
the closed face
the furious death in it
the mouth full of flies and bad breath
dog breath
           murmured a soldier
fatal position
           said a teacher

I'm here:
I embrace your slumped shoulder
your spoiled skin
your slightly sunken cheeks
your long legs with varicose veins and scabs
I give you tremors
attempt to moan like the old
and pray
and cross myself
and light a candle
Saint Vincent that they will not do him more harm
Saint Rosalia and Saint Anthony of Assisi father of the mountains
that they do not find him

THE DAUGHTER

The father wants to die in October because it's the cloudiest month of
      the year
we are diminished
silent and cursed
enveloped in submission and difficulty
He moves himself like a shadow pacing the fire of a high mountain
looking for the town that takes the circus
All Saints' Day
He shakes the ferns with force and the orchids disperse
From the high ceilings jump geckos and black butterflies
I know that joy will arrive out of season like how that crop of sunflowers
could have caught much of the moonlight much of the serenity
The night clears earlier now
Is March not better?
at the hour of every day
when the gardens change the color of the sky?
Still, he does not choose the place
but is thinking already about the extermination of the light
and the worry fills his eyes with tears.

THE GUILT

The object of my guilt is unfathomable
as the smell of mandarins in the garden of my father.
In the first instance
I wanted to be reasonable
to have honest feelings of regret
when cruelty began to take unusual frequency.
Snubbed
my mother condemned me to wander routinely
through irritating cities
where people are pushed against the edge of the sidewalk
and extract their veins to hang in the sun
and extract their eyes to turn into gemstones
and extract their guts to hang from the lampposts
The action was verified:
I was the one with infinite love for humankind
the living guilt of so many torments.

WHAT TO DO WITH THEM?

The man who loves zoos.
The witness of the Beatitudes of the meat.
The woman beat down by exhaustion.
The genuine count who fools the false court.
The beloved—oh how beloved!—of the lunatics.
The passenger who lies to avoid their destination.
The know-it-all teens with their cracking voices.
The one who shelters havens with abuse.
That stranger of March who passes through my house and beckons me to ruin.
The disenchantment of the assassins when there is no breeze.
The melancholy of El Chino, the restlessness of Orlando, the sweetness of Luis Camilo.
The dismemberment of St. Augustine, still hoping for a unanimous decision.
The loneliness of foreign countries.
The epistolary put-downs.
The fallacies of the spiteful.
The pulp novels with happy endings.
The painters enraged when nobody sees.
The possessed cinematographers.
The morning of jasmine and waves when you sleep and love me.
The day all the furies unite.
          What to do with them?

THIS CURSED TERRITORY

After recovering the body
they did not ask me how I was feeling
and the neighbor gave me a few small pats on the neck
there where you usually nosed around before throwing yourself into sleep.
As I promised you,
I keep my legs strong and live upright as the stem of a flower,
and though they say that lemon balm is the leaf of the melancholy,
I breathe it at night
before knowing if there will be frost at dawn.
Of the recommended poetries
I've barely read any.
I try to kill time
time without you
without possibilities of autumns or duck hunts
nor of trips to Canada.
But suddenly
I open my eyes
and I hear my mother calling for an afternoon snack
in the middle of this silence tempering three in the morning.
The man upstairs opens his sliding glass window
spying on the breath of the night like someone with no place to cry
and when it happens
it fills my eyes with tears
I'm obsessed with him
a small matter from balcony to balcony.

I have tried to change this pain with a great tumult
and nevertheless,
I end up content
go and come by the dark living room
without having stopped to install the floor lamp
that would have thrown a golden light about the legs of the invited
There is that book of Hellman's
that you loved so much
because she loved Dash and sent to him by mail a thousand meters of

telephone cable
that they never used.
My hopes are low
but tomorrow I will think only of them.
For now, I curse the mountains the guava marmalade the toothpaste
the cold cream on my cheeks the intersections of avenues
the tree of the house where we moved for the second time
I curse cursed curses for all the stories they whispered at me:
you
lying down
on one side
on a long table
polished dark brown
made from my skin and all my cursed curses.

from THE SMELL, THE STREET, & THE SORROW

Sure, it's beautiful to re-read. But somebody wrote it and that somebody was you. Fuck women's poetry and the two days of labor that serve to help you scripturally weep. Word out of bounds. Of context. You don't like either of the two. Well, there you go. A bunch of writing for nothing. Poets are like that. They write two lines and ejaculate. Alone. They love all that they write. Instead, look at you. You are a poet and you don't ejaculate. Something that is an unforgivable fault.

Look at this poem, isn't it lovely?

Move your tongue seven times before speaking
said the big when one was small
and sucked
       mother
            land
                   tit
                         lime
                                wood
                                        hair
                                              lace
But we knew that no age would last forever
and so
life had passed
with her seventy-five beats
perfect frequency of sadness

That's what you have right now: seventy-five pulsations. Normal. And you cling to these beats, as if your life depended upon it. What would your friend Federico say? Once he insinuated that you stick your nose where it doesn't belong. That's why your heart beats so hard. Poor Federico! If he only knew that my nose is connected to my heart and my heart to my mouth and my heart to my stomach and my heart to my belly and my belly to my stomach. If you re-read it yourself now, you would feel great shame. You're writing for the moral. Not for you. Great discourses, great lines, great oaths of I did not go. Nobody is to blame. Except you. And you really have it. Like all the poets have always had it, heard in some damn sorrow that does not exist. But when they do write, it's not for nothing. This poem of yours is a great proof of that.

*   *   *

I don't have years to wake up tomorrow
and to encounter the flowering blood of a heart of the street
Will they be reasonable, those who dispute my bones behind the door?
I don't have to mourn.
What I still like
I think about with my eyes closed,
walk it timidly
and with giant fear.
It's forbidden to put life on the table
and would in no way serve
to be enchanted by the scent of a carnation.
Invented in mirrors
the voices of my guilt. There they are: with all teeth bared.

You're sweating. You're tired. How many times are you going to conduct yourself with impunity? cutting the light of the blinds with your silhouette

that make the day unbearable
Cast out
I fear for the habits of life
They are in the walls
the dusty shelves
the unhinged door
the avenue that goes down to the city
who can be warned now of the signs of horror?

Keep on thinking you write well. That's your biggest concern. You re-read and can't find anything wrong. Except that you don't like it.
Well, William Blake isn't convincing either. Nor Dylan Thomas.
Confess it: reading poetry is a boring duty most of the time.
You get tired. But you don't dare write a novel. You rebel:
Isn't all this poetry?

Keep on with your tedious revisions. Go on, little word!

Will you stay awhile?
I'll stay
until you tell me your latest dream
Do not be afraid of the calm that surrounds
or the rustle of the freshly washed silk
Do not make appetites of this hopelessness
of this simple misfortune
I'll stay
until they come for us.

Dear Mama,

all the world strives to demonstrate to me the utility of mothers. I set off to slander this with increasingly lewd gestures. I don't share the thesis of a fireplace and a warm hand in the lap. You take it from here, at night when the apartment is full of shadows. I chase you with a broom and a stick, but you always flee through the crack of the bathroom window. It's so much fun!

A blood all mine, running from moon to moon, with an eyelid closed under a tranquil hand. I looked at him and my eyes filled with tears. He likes Reverdy, Breton, Perret, Lautreamont. I hate that gang of surreal and automatic cruelty. In the hours I am permitted, I am reborn before the wetness, I rub against Rafael's virgin and perk up my ears at the fountains of Bernini. On my knees, I let myself be enveloped by the waters of Botticelli. Under the direction of an accusatory finger, I have read *Nadja* and *The Thief of Children*. But a simple misfortune returned me to the signs of horror. I murmur then, as now, obscenities and stick my tongue out at the mirror. Move your tongue in your mouth seven times before speaking. I was remembering that biblical and familial caution and I was taking between my lips the mystery of the dead sex, asleep, until it's obligated to wake, surprised by this unique gesture of fate. I feel behind my back the soft sound of a loose breath, morbid, all of a sudden alone in the middle of this disorder of cloth and wool tangled around my feet. The rumors of my heart, scandalous, disturbing, no longer disquiet me. I want that hapless look about his nape and I hope they beat him to death, I hope to feel the heat of my own blood running in a burning and painful thread to the narrow sides of my legs, the insides.

Those who write are not even of a race. Nor a caste. Nor a class. Nor are they one. They ruin the point of living, like women in a world of science. Behind thick lenses, the court is never dull. They have all privileges: from philosophy up to anger, passing through conjugal relations, and the length of the paragraphs. Between the rights of man it is figured that the writer should write largely for himself first, then for the others, with a purpose well or poorly defined: to flood the window displays, walls, countries, homes. Or, when all is said and done, to commit suicide.

For poetry, cursed and hated, there is always a day that follows: death. What can be taught from an atomic explosion but the agony of those most dispossessed and the infernal laugh of the idiot prophets? The fire is no surprise to the poets. The fire is part of those who, day by day, gamble their lives on the horror of solitude.

For them, a stupid way of living.

For them, there is no way of living. Gerard de Nerval hanged himself in an alley as dark as it was light, it was a field of corn in Kansas City. Baudelaire slowly opened his veins so his friend wouldn't feel scared when he was gone. Cesar Vallejo agonized because it was cold and he couldn't accept just how cold it was. Cesare Pavese knelt atop the most beautiful hills in Italy to ask death to come and he had eyes of fire. Distant, more distant still, the ghosts that detained Ulysses momentarily confirmed today their profound and true reason: not wanting to return.

There is in The next day a power.
There is in the images of The next day a power that is not of critics, not of publicists, not of politicians, they will never understand. It is the power of those who do not have anything, save their sweet waiting for the end. They are the silent nothing. Those that welcome the fire like a logical inheritance from a traitorous memory.

There is in the images of The next day a power that is not of critics, not of publicists, not of politicians, they can't understand, not now, not ever. It is the power of the silent nothing. It is the power of those who don't have anything and accept the fire like a logical inheritance from the past.

It is the power of the silent nothing. They are neither the majority, nor minority.

They are there: trapped by the same fire that created them.

Trapped in a familiar fire. There is no surprise for those who day by day gamble life on the horror of solitude, of isolation, of those tiny brightnesses, of those small squalors.

It is the power of the silent nothing. They are neither the majority, nor minority. They are there: trapped by the fire. They feel neither surprise nor astonishment. Day by day, they had gambled life in the horror of solitude, of isolation, of squalor. With them, life disappears once and for all.

ANGER, lord,
               it's only anger
that makes me go back to the city.
This town, lord,
               this one horse town
godforsaken town that no one should name.
It was an obligation to run there
                         to scream and to sing
to fall down on the mossy stone
          slippery
                              fetid
to sink oneself into the mercy of the sky
                              above
situated in the map keys of the unique navigator who arrived
                                        and departed
nauseated by this town, lord,
                    I swear it.
nauseated.

One day
you will be
the girl with the slumped shoulders.
Do not try
then
nothing
out
of the ordinary.

I feel bad,
I would like to have lighter hair,
a softer voice,
big and clear eyes,
strong and flexible legs,
I feel bad.

I invent shouts, screams, revolts
but generally people flee
or they remain silent.
And always,
at this time,
I'm dying of anger, of sleep.

That
of looking for someone,
of remembering them,
of finding them,
of not finding them,
it means something when it's December
and there's wind outside
and there's cold outside
and there's silence outside.

All the time
the jaw
ready to chew the lip
rosy
bleeding
biting
howling
twisting me
suddenly lifting me
trying to be a shadow much taller
much longer
the cypress that crowds my infancy
leans over me
occupies itself with me
looks over me
is silent for me
crunches the meat torn apart by my nails
disregards all pain
it's my meat
hated meat
thought of like meat
victim
executioner
there is not a happy point on the stairs of Siena
defiance at the moment of dying.

THE LAST TREMOR of the once visited cities
fragile concise vision of the trees that encircle
the hand resting on the ground
dust that fills the eyes,
cry to the end
of the triumphant encounter.
A special future,
infuriating teenager, reserved for you
mother sweet to touch and smell,
what will there be behind the mountain where the birds sing day and
      night?
Why does the water run with that noise of blood and us listening,
      montionless,
scared, victims of our own ambushes?
mother
sweet to touch and smell
lost in thick sheets of linen
useless and superfluous
across a lifetime
someday I would have been able to look at you again
without compassion nor contemplation.

WHAT YOU write,
it's not poetry
No.
No it's not.
Clearly you have many particular ideas about poetry.
A flash of light on the sea.
Time arrested.
The curve of a shoulder.

Nobody hears it.
Or pretends not to hear it.
Or heard it but did not understand it.
Or definitely,
not me.

When someone says, I'm fed up, it's commonplace.
When someone premeditates a crime, it's original.
Both things, however, are commonplaces.
There's more.
Unsustainable solitudes like this.
With petty questions, like,
why her and not me,
why him and not me,
and no one has the delicate suspicion of Virginia Woolf
to speak between lines of frustration.
Virginia killed herself.
Not just me.
Through the wall it's possible to hear it all.
Yes, all.
Maybe the scratching of dragged furniture,
or the laughs of children who never end up sleeping.
I know I'm judged because I don't dream.
They make me laugh, those who brag about their enormous
capacity to make art.
More than an idiot who tells you to dream in a placid suburb
of the capital.
Or in a horrible and hot tropical town.
Or in a chilly village of the north.
I've always heard the same phrase when I get
angry:
there's something you haven't said,
apparently,
what I answer:
Are you that scared?
I couldn't lock eyes with the stranger.
Strange because the night before he had made love to me.

I don't know why he thought that I was scared.
Squatting on the bidet,
I could only recall photographs of an actress with cancer.
But that
doesn't mean I was scared.
Besides,
when I returned to bed
he was asleep.
Snoring face up.
Ever so gently
I placed him on his side
and he continued sleeping.
Touched him.
and he did not wake.
This bird who always sings at the same hour
it's the only thing that scares me.
Doing it on purpose.
Trying to wake him
when I know
all he wants is to sleep.

El objeto de mi culpa

es insondable.

Tiene olor a mandarinas

a puerco degollado

a hierro batido

a gacelas del oeste medio.

Una ondada de lluvia

                golpea el ciprés

y estoy

cara a la oscuridad.

Con el puño

levanto mi piel.

La saliva pasa

entre piedras de ríos

y caracoles de Borgoña/

desborda mi piel

el otro lado

de la vigilia.

Miyó Vestrini was born in France, 1938, emigrated to Venezuela at the age of 9, and at eighteen she joined Apocalipsis (Apocalypse), the only woman to do so in the then male-dominated scene of the Venezuelan literary avant-garde. She soon became a dedicated and prize-winning journalist, directing the arts section of the newspaper *El Nacional*. She published three books of poetry in her lifetime: 1971's *Las historias de Giovanna* (*The Stories of Giovanna*), 1975's *El invierno próximo* (*Next Winter*), and *Pocas virtudes* (*Little Virtues*), published in 1986. Vestrini died by suicide on November 29, 1991, leaving behind two collections: a book of poems, *Valiente Ciudadano* (*Brave Citizen*) and a book of stories, *Órdenes al corazón* (*Orders to the Heart*).

Anne Boyer is a U.S. poet and essayist whose books include *A Handbook of Disappointed Fate* (2018) and the CLMP award-winning *Garments Against Women* (2015). In 2018, Boyer received the inaugural Cy Twombly Award from the Foundation for Contemporary Arts and a Whiting Award in poetry and nonfiction. She is the 2018-19 Judith E. Wilson Fellow in poetry at Cambridge University and an associate professor of the liberal arts at the Kansas City Art Institute.

Cassandra Gillig is an archivist and liturgical poet working under the New Order of St. Agatha. She is at work on a book of correspondence between Diane di Prima and Audre Lorde and a middle grade book about animal liberation and the end of Amazon. She lives in Kansas City.

Faride Mereb is a Venezuelan editor and book designer currently living in New York City and specializing in typography. She is the founder and director of the publishing house Ediciones Letra Muerta, based in Caracas, Venezuela. In 2016 she was awarded gold in the editorial category in the Latin American Design Awards for *Al Filo ~ Miyó Vestrini*.

Published by Kenning Editions
3147 W Logan Blvd., Suite 7, Chicago, IL 60647

Kenningeditions.com

Distributed by Small Press Distribution
1341 Seventh St., Berkeley, CA 94710

Spdbooks.org

This book was made possible in part by the supporters of Kenning
Editions: Charles Bernstein, Julietta Cheung, Carol Ciavonne, Steve
Dickison, Craig Dworkin, Kristin Dykstra, Laura Elrick, Jais Gossman,
Kaplan Harris, Tom Healy, Lyn Hejinian, Kevin Killian, Edward McAdams,
Krishan Mistry, Dee Morris, Chris Muravez, Sawako Nakayasu, Caroline
Picard, Janelle Rebel, Kit Robinson, Jesse Seldess, Tyrone Williams, and
Steven Zultanski.

Kenning Editions is a 501c3 non-profit, independent literary publisher
investigating the relationships of aesthetic quality to political commit-
ment. Consider donating or subscribing: Kenningeditions.com/shop/
donation

KENNING EDITIONS